CALIFOR
NATIVE AMERIC

CHUMASH TRIBE

WITHDRAWN

by
Mary Null Boulé

Illustrated by
Daniel Liddell

CONTRA COSTA COUNTY LIBRARY
Merryant Publishers, Inc.
Vashon, WA 98070
206-463-3879

Book Number Four in a series of twenty-eight

This series is dedicated to Virginia Harding, whose editing expertise and friendship brought this project to fruition.

Library of Congress Catalog Card Number: 92-61897
ISBN: 1-877599-28-X

Copyright © 1992, Merryant Publishing

7615 S.W. 257th St., Vashon, WA 98070.

FOREWORD

Native American people of the United States are often living their lives away from major cities and away from what we call the mainstream of life. It is, then, interesting to learn of the important part these remote tribal members play in our everyday lives.

More than 60% of our foods come from the ancient Native American's diet. Farming methods of today also can be traced back to how tribal women grew crops of corn and grain. Many of our present day ideas of democracy have been taken from tribal governments. Even some 1,500 Native American words are found in our English language today.

Fur traders bought furs from tribal hunters for small amounts of money, sold them to Europeans and Asians for a great deal of money, and became rich. Using their money to buy land and to build office buildings, some traders started business corporations which are now the base of our country's economy.

There has never been enough credit given to these early Americans who took such good care of our country when it was still in their care. The time has come to realize tribal contributions to our society today and to give Native Americans not only the credit, but the respect due them.

Mary Boulé

A-frame cradle for girls; tule matting. Tubatulabal tribe.

GENERAL INFORMATION

Creation legends told by today's tribal people speak of how, very long ago, their creator placed them in a territory, where they became caretakers of that land and its animals. None of their ancient legends tells about the first Native Americans coming from another continent.

It is important to respect the different beliefs and theories, to learn from and seek the truth in all of them.

Villagers' tribal history lessons do not agree with the beliefs of anthropologists (scientific historians who study the habits and customs of humans).

Clues found by these scientists lead them to believe that ancient tribespeople came to North America from Asia during the Ice Age period some 20 to 35 thousand years ago. They feel these humans walked over a land strip in the Bering Straits, following animal herds who provided them with food.

Scientists' understanding of ancient people must come from studying clues; for example, tools, utensils, baskets, garbage discoveries, and stories they passed from one generation to the next.

California's Native Americans did not organize into large tribes. Instead they divided into tribelets, sometimes having as many as 250 people. Some tribelets had only one chief for each village.

From 20 to 100 people could be living in one village, which usually had several houses. In most cases, these groups of people were one family and were related to each other. From five to ten people of a family might live in one house. For instance, a mother, a father, two or three children, a grandmother, or aunt or daughter-in-law might live together.

Village members together would own the land important to them for their well-being. Their land might include oak trees with precious acorns, streams and rivers, and plants which were good to eat. Streams and rivers were especially important to a tribe's quality of life. Water drew animals to it; that meant more food for the tribe to eat. Fish were a good source of food, and traveling by boat was often easier than walking long distances. Water was needed in every part of tribal life.

Village and tribelet land was carefully guarded. Each group knew exactly where the boundaries of its land were found. Boundaries were known by landmarks such as mountains or rivers, or they might also be marked by poles planted in the ground. Some boundary lines were marked by rocks, or by objects placed there by tribal members. The size of a territory had to be large enough to supply food to every person living there.

The California tribes spoke many languages. Sometimes villages close together even had a problem understanding one another. This meant that each group had to be sure of the boundaries of other tribes around them when gathering food. It would not be wise to go against the boundaries and the customs of neighbors. The Native Americans found if they respected the boundaries of their neighbors, not so many wars had to be fought. California tribes, in spite of all their differences, were not as warlike as other tribes in our country.

Not only did the California tribes speak different languages, but their members also differed in size. Some tribes were very tall, almost six feet tall. The shortest people came from the Yuki tribe which had territory in what is now Mendocino County. They measured only about 5'2" tall. All Native Americans, regardless of size, had strong, straight black hair and dark brown eyes.

TRADE

Trading between tribes was an important part of life. Inland tribes had large animal hides that coastal tribes wanted. By trading the hides to coastal groups, inland tribes would receive fish and shells, which they in turn wanted. Coastal tribes also wanted minerals and rocks mined in the mountains by inland tribes. Obsidian rock from the northern mountains was especially wanted for arrowheads. There were, as well, several minerals, mined in the inland mountains, which could be made into the colorful body paints needed for religious ceremonies.

Southern tribes particularly wanted steatite from the Gabrielino tribe. Steatite, or soapstone, was a special metal which allowed heat to spread evenly through it. This made it a good choice to be used for cooking pots and flat frying pans. It could be carved into bowls because of its softness and could be decorated by carving designs into it. Steatite came from Catalina Island in the Coastal Gabrielino territory. Gabrielinos found steatite to be a fine trading item to offer for the acorns, deerskins, or obsidian stone they needed.

When people had no items to trade but needed something, they used small strings of shells for money. The small dentalium shells, which came from the far distant Northwest coast, had great value. Strings of dentalia usually served as money in the Northern California tribes, although some dentalia was used in the Central California tribes.

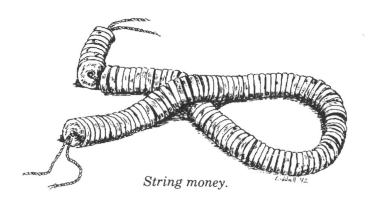

String money.

In southern California clam shells were broken and holes were bored through the center of each piece. Then the pieces were rounded and polished with sandstone and strung into strings for money. These were not thought to be as valuable as dentalia.

Strings of shell money were measured by tattoo marks on the trader's lower arm or hand.

Here is a sample of shell value:

> A house, three strings
> A fishing place, one to three strings
> Land with acorn-bearing oak trees, one to five strings

A great deal of rock and stone was traded among the tribes for making tools. Arrows had to have sharp-edged stone for tips. The best stone for arrow tips was obsidian (volcanic glass) because, when hit properly, it broke off into flakes with very sharp edges. California tribes considered obsidian to be the most valuable rock for trading.

Some tribes had craftsmen who made knives with wooden handles and obsidian blades. Often the handles were decorated with carvings. Such knives were good for trading purposes. Stone mortars and pestles, used by the women for grinding grains into flour, were good trading items.

BASKETS & POTTERY

California tribal women made beautiful baskets. The Pomo and Chumash baskets, what few are left, show us that the women of those tribes might have been some of the finest basketmakers in the world. Baskets were used for gathering and storing food, for carrying babies, and even for hauling water. In emergencies, such as flooding waters, sometimes children, women, and tribal belongings crossed the swollen rivers and streams in huge, woven baskets! Baskets were so tightly woven that not a drop of water could leak from them.

Baskets also made fine cooking pots. Very hot rocks were taken from a fire and tossed around inside baskets with a looped tree branch until food in the basket was cooked.

Most baskets were made to do a certain job, but some baskets were designed for their beauty alone and were excellent for trading. Older women of a tribe would teach young girls how to weave baskets.

Pottery was not used by many California tribes. What little there was seems to have been made by those tribes living near to the Navaho and Mohave tribes of Arizona, and it shows their style. For example, pottery of the California tribes did not have much decoration and was usually a dull red color. Designs were few and always in yellow.

Ohlone hunter wearing deerskin camouflage.

Long thin coils of clay were laid one on top the other. Then the coils were smoothed between a wooden paddle and a small stone to shape the bowl. Pottery from California Native Americans has been described as light weight and brittle (easily broken), probably because of the kind of clay soil found in California.

HUNTING & FISHING

Tribal men spent much of their time making hunting and fishing tools. Bows and arrows were built with great care, to make them shoot as accurately as possible. Carelessly made hunting weapons caused fewer animals to be killed and people then had less food to eat.

Bows made by men of Southern California tribes were made long and narrow. In the northern part of the state bows were a little shorter, thinner, and wider than those of their northern neighbors. Size and thickness of bows depended on the size trees growing in a tribe's territory. The strongest bows were wrapped with sinew, the name given to animal tendons. Sinew is strong and elastic like a rubber band.

Arrows were made in many sizes and shapes, depending on their use. For hunting larger animals, a two-piece arrow was used. The front piece of the arrow shaft was made so that it would remain in the animal, even if the back part was removed or broken off. The arrowhead, or point, was wrapped to the front piece of the shaft. This kind of arrow was also used in wars.

Young boys used a simple wooden arrow with the end sharpened to a point. With this they could hunt small animals like birds and rabbits. The older men of the tribe taught boys how to make their own arrows, how to aim properly, and how to repair broken weapons.

Tribal men spent many hours making and mending fishing nets. The string used in making nets often came from the fibers of plants. These fibers were twisted to make them strong and tough, then knotted into netting. Fences, or weirs, that had one small opening for fish, were built across streams. As the fish swam through the opening they would be caught in netting or harpooned by a waiting fisherman.

Hooks, if used at all, were cut from shells. Mostly hooks could be found when the men fished in large lakes or when catching trout in high mountain areas. Hooks were attached to heavy plant fiber string.

Dip nets, made of netting attached to branches that were bent into a circle, were used to catch fish swimming near shore. Dip nets had long handles so the fishermen could reach deep into the water.

Sometimes a mild poison was placed on the surface of shallow water. This confused the fish and caused them to float to the surface of the water, where they could be scooped up by a waiting fisherman. Not enough poison was used to make humans ill.

Not all fishing was done from the shore. California tribes used two kinds of boats when fishing. Canoes, dug out of one half a log, were useful for river fishing. These were square at each end, round on the bottom, and very heavy. Some of them were well-finished, often even having a carved seat in them.

Today we think of "balsa" as a very lightweight wood, but in Spanish, the word balsa means "raft". That is why Spanish explorers called the Native American canoes, made from tule reeds, "balsa" boats.

Balsa boats were made of bundled tule reeds and were used throughout most of California. They made into safe, light-weight boats for lake and river use. Usually the balsa canoe had a long, tightly tied bundle of tule for the boat bottom and one bundle for each side of the canoe. The front of the canoe was higher than the back. Balsa boats could be steered with a pole or with a paddle, like a raft.

Men did most of the fishing, women were in charge of gathering grasses, seeds, and acorns for food. After the food was collected, it was either eaten right away or made ready for winter storage.

Except for a few southern groups, California tribes had permanent villages where they lived most of the year. They also had food-gathering places they returned to each year to collect acorns, salt, fish, and other foods not found near their villages.

FOOD

Many different kinds of plant food grew wild in California in the days before white people arrived. Berries and other plant foods grew in the mountains. Forests offered the local tribes everything from pine nuts to animals.

Native Americans found streams full of fish for much of the year. Inland fresh water lakes had large tule reeds growing along their shores. Tule could be eaten as food when plants were young and tender. More important,

tule

11

however, tule was used in making fabric for clothes and for building boats and houses. Tule was probably the most useful plant the California Native Americans found growing wild in their land.

Like all deserts, the one in southern California had little water or fish, but small animals and cactus plants made good food for the local tribes. They moved from place to place harvesting whatever was ripe. Tribal members always knew when and where to find the best food in their territory.

Acorns were the main source of food for all California tribes. Acorn flour was as important to the California Native Americans as wheat is to us today. Five types of California oak trees produced acorns that could be eaten. Those from black oak and tanbark oak seem to have been the favorite kinds.

Since some acorns tasted better than others, the tastiest ones were collected first. If harvest of the favorite acorn was poor some years, then less tasty acorns had to be eaten all winter long.

So important were acorns to California Indians that most tribes built their entire year around them. Acorn harvest marked the beginning of their calendar year. Winter was counted as so many months after acorn harvest, and summer was counted by the number of months before the next acorn harvest.

Acorn harvest ceremonies usually were the biggest events of the year. Most celebrations took place in mid-October and included dancing, feasts, games of chance, and reunions with relatives. Harvest festivals lasted for many days. They were a time of joy for everyone.

The annual acorn gathering lasted two to three weeks. Young boys climbed the oak trees to shake branches; some men used long poles to knock acorns to the ground. Women loaded the nuts into large cone-shaped burden baskets and carried them to a central place where they were put in the sun to dry.

Once the acorns were dried, the women carried them back to the tribe's permanent villages. There they lined special basket-like storage granaries with strong herbs to keep insects away, then stored the acorns inside. Granaries were placed on stilts to keep animals from getting into them and were kept beside tribal houses.

Preparing acorns for each meal was also the women's job. Shells were peeled by hitting the acorns with a stone hammer on an anvil (flat) stone. Meat from the nut was then laid on a stone mortar. A mortar was usually a large stone with a slight dip on its surface. Sometimes the mortar had a bottomless basket, called a hopper, glued to its top. This kept the acorn meat from sliding off the mortar as it was beaten. The meat was then pounded with a long stone pestle. Acorn flour was scraped away from the hopper's sides with a soaproot fiber brush during this process.

From there the flour was put into an open-worked basket and sifted. A fine flour came through the bottom of the basket, while the larger pieces were put back in the mortar for more pounding.

The most important process came after the acorn flour was sifted. Acorn flour has a very bitter-tasting tannin in it. This bitter taste was removed by a method called leaching. Many tribes leached the flour by first scooping out a hollow in sand near water. The hollow was lined with leaves to keep the flour from washing away. A great deal of hot water was poured through the flour to wash out (leach) the bitterness. Sometimes the flour was put into a basket for the leaching process, instead of using sand and leaves.

Finally the acorn flour was ready to be cooked. To make mush, heated stones were placed in the basket with the flour. A looped tree branch or two long sticks were used to toss the hot rocks around so the basket would not burn. When the mush had boiled, it could be eaten. If the flour and water mixture was baked in an earthen oven, it became a kind of bread. Early explorers wrote that it was very tasty.

Historians have estimated that one family would eat from 1500 to 2000 pounds of acorn flour a year. One reason California native Americans did not have to plant seeds and raise crops was because there were so many acorns for them to harvest each year.

Whether they ate fish or shellfish or plant food or animal meat, nature supplied more than enough food for the Native Americans who lived in California long ago. Many believed their good fortune in having fine weather and plenty to eat came from being good to their gods.

RELIGION

Tribal members had strong beliefs in the power of spirits or gods around them. Each tribe was different, but all felt the importance of never making a spirit angry with them. For that reason a celebration to thank the spirit-gods for treating them well, took place before each food gathering and before each hunting trip, and after each food harvest.

Usually spiritual powers were thought to belong to birds or animals. Most California tribespeople felt bears were very wicked and should not be eaten. But Coyote seems to have been a kind leader who helped them if they were in trouble, even though he seems to have been a bit naughty at times. Eagle was thought to be very powerful and good to native Americans. In some tribes, Eagle was almost as powerful as Sun.

Tribes placed importance on different gods, according to the tribe's needs. Rain gods were the most important spirits to desert tribes. Weather gods, who might bring less rain or warmer temperatures, were important to northern tribes. A great many groups felt there were gods for each of the winds: North, South, East and West. The four directions were usually included in their ceremonial dances and were used as part of the decorations on baskets, pots, and even tools.

Animals were not only worshipped and believed to be spirit-gods, like Deer or Antelope, but tribal members felt there was a personal animal guardian for each one of them. If a tribal member had a deer as guardian, then that person could never kill a deer or eat deer meat.

California Native Americans believed in life after death. This made them very respectful of death and very fearful of angering a dead person. Once someone died, the name of the dead person could never again be said aloud. Since it was easy to accidentally say a name aloud, the name was usually given to a new baby. Then the dead person would not become angry.

Shamans were thought to be the keepers of religious beliefs and to have the ability to talk directly to spirit-gods. It was the job of a village shaman to cure sick people, and to speak to the gods about the needs of the people. Some tribes had several kinds of shamans in one village. One shaman did curing, one scared off evil spirits, while another took care of hunters.

Not all shamans were nice, so people greatly feared their power. However, if shamans had no luck curing sick people or did not bring good luck in hunting, the people could kill them. Most shamans were men, but in a few tribes, women were doctors.

Most California tribal myths have been lost to history because they were spoken and never written down. The legends were told and retold on winter nights around the home fires. Sadly, these were forgotten after the missionaries brought Christianity to California and moved tribal members into the missions.

A few stories still remain, however. It is thought by historians that northwest California tribes were the only ones not to have a myth on how they were created. They did not feel that the world was made and prepared for human beings. Instead, their few remaining stories usually tell of mountain peaks or rivers in their own territory.

The central California tribes had creation stories of a great flood where there was only water on earth. They tell of how man was made from a bit of mud that a turtle brought up from the bottom of the water.

Many southwest tribes believed there was a time of no sky or water. They told of two clouds appearing which finally became Sky and Earth.

Throughout California, however, all tribes had myths that told of Eagle as the leader, Coyote as chief assistant, and of less powerful spirits like Falcon or Hawk.

Costumes for religious ceremonies often imitated these animals they worshipped or feared. Much time was spent in making the dance costumes as beautiful as possible. Red woodpecker feathers were so brilliant a color they were used to decorate religious headdresses, necklaces, or belts. Deerskin clothing was fringed so shell beads could be attached to each thin strip of leather.

Eagle feathers were felt to be the most sacred of religious objects. Sometimes they were made into whole robes.

Religious feather charm.

Usually, though, the feathers were used just for decorations. All these costumes were valuable to the people of each tribe. The village chief was in charge of taking care of the costumes, and there was terrible punishment for stealing them. Clothing worn everyday was not fancy like costuming for rituals.

Willow bark skirt.

CLOTHING

Central and southern California's fine weather made regular clothes not really very important to the Native Americans. The children and men went naked most of the year, but most women wore a short apron-like skirt. These skirts were usually made in two pieces, front and back aprons, with fringes cut into the bottom edges. Often the skirt was made from the inner bark of trees, shredded and gathered on a cord. Sometimes the skirt was made from tule or grass.

In northern California and in rainy or windy weather elsewhere in the state, animal-skin blankets were worn by both men and women. They were used like a cape and wrapped around the body. Sometimes the cape was put over one shoulder and under the other arm, then tied in front. All kinds of skins were used; deer, otter, wildcat, but sea-otter fur was thought to be the best. If the skin was from a small animal, it was cut into strips and woven together into a fabric. At night the cape became a blanket to keep the person warm.

Because of the rainy weather in northern California, the women wore basket caps all the time. Women of the central and south tribes wore caps only when carrying heavy loads, where the forehead had to be used as support. Then a cap helped keep too much weight from being placed on the forehead.

Most California people went barefoot in their villages. For journeys into rough land, going to war, wood gathering, or in colder weather, the tribesmen in central and northwest California wore a one-piece soft shoe with no extra sole, which went high up on the leg.

Southern California tribespeople, however, wore sandals most of the time, wearing high, soled moccasins only when they traveled long distances or into the mountains. Leggings of skin were worn in snow, and moccasins were sometimes lined with grass for more comfort and warmth.

VILLAGE LIFE

Houses of the California tribes were made of materials found in their area. Usually they were round with domed roofs. Except for a few tribes, a house floor was dug into the earth a few feet. This was wise, for it made the home warmer in winter and cooler in summer. It also meant that less material was needed to make house walls.

Framework for the walls was made from bendable branches tied to support poles. Some frames of the houses were covered with earth and grass. Others were covered with large slabs of redwood or pine bark. Central California

Split-stick clapper, rhythm instrument. Hupa tribe.

villagers made large woven mats of tule reed to cover the tops and sides of houses. In the warmer southern area, brush and smaller pieces of bark were used for house walls.

Most California Native American villages had a building called a sweathouse, where the men could be found when they were not hunting, fishing or traveling. It was a very important place for the men, who used it rather like a clubhouse. They could sweat and then scrape themselves clean with curved ribs of deer. The sweathouse was smaller than a family house. Normally it had a center pole framework with a firepit on the ground next to the pole. When the fire was lit, some smoke was allowed to escape through a hole at the top of the roof; however, most was trapped inside the building. Smoke and heat were the main reasons for having a sweathouse. Both were believed to be a way to purify tribal members' bodies. Sweathouse walls were mainly hard-packed earth. The heat produced was not a steam heat but came from a wood-fed fire.

In the center of most villages was a large house that often had no walls, just a roof held up with poles. It was here that religious dances and rituals were held, or visitors were entertained.

Dances were enjoyed and were performed with great skill. Music, usually only rhythm instruments, accompanied the dances. For some reason California Native Americans did not use drums to create rhythms for their dances. Three different kinds of rattles were used by California tribes.

One type, split-clap sticks, created rhythm for dancing. These were usually a length of cane (a hollow stick) split in half lengthwise for about two-thirds of its length. The part still uncut was tightly wound with cord so it would not split all the way. The stick was held at the tied end in one hand and hit against the palm of the other hand to make its sound.

A pebble-filled moth cocoon made rhythm for shaman duties. These could range from calling on spirits to cure illnesses, to performing dances to bring rain. Probably the best sounds to beat rhythm for songs and dances came from bundles of deer hooves tied together on a stick. These rattles have a hollow, warm sound.

The only really "musical" instrument found in California was a flute made of reed that was played by blowing across the edge of one end. Melodies were not played on any of these instruments. Most North American Indians sang their songs rather than playing melodies on music instruments.

Special songs were sung for each event. There were songs for healing sick people, songs for success in hunting, war, or marriage. Women sang acorn-grinding songs and lullabies. Songs were sung in sorrow for the dead and during story-telling times. Group singing, with a leader, was the favorite kind of singing. Most songs were sung by all tribe members, but religious songs had to be sung by a special group. It was important that sacred songs not be changed through the years. If a mistake was made while singing sacred music, the singer could be punished, so only specially trained singers would sing ritual songs.

All songs were very short, some of them only 20 to 30 seconds long. They were made longer by repeating the melodies over and over, or by connecting several songs together. Songs usually told no story, just repeated words or phrases or syllables in patterns.

Song melodies used only one or two notes and harmony was never added. Perhaps that is why mission Indians, at those missions with musician priests, especially loved to sing harmony in the church choirs.

Songs and dances were good methods of passing rich tribal traditions on to the children. It was important to tribal adults that their children understand and love the tribe's heritage.

Children were truly wanted by parents in most tribes and new parents carefully watched their tiny babies day and night, to be sure they stayed warm and dry. Usually a newborn was strapped into a cradle and tied to the mother's back so she could continue to work, yet be near the baby at all times. In some tribes, older children took care of babies of cradle age during the day to give the mother time to do all her work, while grandmothers were often in charge of caring for toddlers.

Children were taught good behavior, traditions, and tribal rules from babyhood, although some tribes were stricter than others. Most of the time parents made their children obey. Young children could be lightly punished, but in many tribes those over six or seven years old were more severely punished if they did not follow the rules.

Just as children do today, Native American youngsters had childhood traditions they followed. For instance, one tribal tradition said that when a baby tooth came out, a child waited until dusk, faced the setting sun and threw the tooth to the west. There is no mention of a generous tooth fairy, however.

Tribal parents were worried that their offspring might not be strong and brave. Some tribes felt one way to make their children stronger was by forcing them to bathe in ice cold water, even in wintertime. Every once in a while, for example, Modoc children were awakened from sleep and taken to a cold lake or stream for a freezing bath.

But if freezing baths at night were hard on young Native Americans, their days were carefree and happy. Children were allowed to play all day, and some tribes felt children did not even have to come to dinner if they didn't want to. In those tribes, children could come to their houses to eat anytime of the day.

The games boys played are not too different from those played today. Swimming, hide and seek among the tule reeds, a form of tetherball with a mud ball tied to a pole, and willow-javelin throwing kept boys busy throughout the day.

Fathers made their sons small bows and arrows, so boys spent much time trying to improve their hunting skills. They practised shooting at frogs or chipmunks. The first animal any boy killed was not touched or eaten by him. Others would carry the kill home to be cooked and eaten by villagers. This tradition taught boys always to share food.

Another hunting tool for boys was a hollowed-out willow branch. This became like a modern day beanshooter, only the Native American boys shot juniper berries instead of beans. Slingshots made good hunting weapons, as well.

Girls and boys shared many games, but girls playing with each other had contests to see who could make a basket the fastest, or they played with dolls made of tule. Together, young boys and girls played a type of ring-around-the-rosie game, climbed mountains, or built mud houses.

As children grew older, the boys followed their fathers and the girls followed their mothers as the adults did their daily work. Children were not trained in the arts of hunting or basketmaking, however, until they became teenagers.

HISTORY

Spanish missionaries, led by Fray Junipero Serra, arrived in California in 1769 to build missions along the coast of California. By 1823, fifty years later, 21 missions had been founded. Almost all of them were very successful, and the Franciscan monks who ran them were proud of how many Native Americans became Christians.

However, all was not as the monks had planned it would be. Native American people had never been around the diseases European white men brought with them. As a result, they had no immunity to such illnesses as measles, small pox, or flu. Too many mission Indians died from white men's diseases.

Historians figure there were 300,000 Native Americans living in California before the missionaries came. The missions show records of 83,000 mission Indians during mission days. By the time the Mexicans took over the missions from the Spanish in 1834, only 20,000 remained alive.

The great California Gold Rush of 1849 was probably another big reason why many of the Native Americans died during that time. White men, staking their claim to tribal lands with gold upon it, thought nothing of killing any California tribesman who tried to keep and protect his territory. Fifty-thousand tribal members died from diseases, bullets, or starvation between the gold Rush Days and 1870. By 1910, only 17,000 California Indians remained.

Although the American government tried to set aside reservations (areas reserved for Native Americans), the land given to the Indians often was not good land. Worse yet, some of the land sacred to tribes, such as burial grounds, was taken over by white people and never given back.

Sadly, mission Indians, when they became Christians, forgot the proud heritage and beliefs they had followed for thousands of years. Many wonderful myths and songs they had passed from one generation to the next, on winter nights so long ago, have been lost forever.

Today some 100,000 people can claim California Native American ancestors, but few pure-blooded tribespeople remain. Our link with the Wanderers, who came from Asia so long ago, has been forever broken.

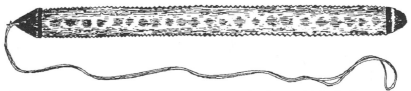

The bullroarer made a deep, loud sound when whirled above the player's head. Tipai tribe.

Villages were usually built beside a lake, stream, or river. Balsa canoes are on the shore. Tule reeds grow along the edge of the water and are drying on poles on the right side of the picture.

Women preparing food in baskets, sit on tule mats. Tule mats are being tied to the willow pole framework of a house being built by one of the men.

THE CHUMASH TRIBE

The Chumash (Choo' mah sh) tribe was large and had one of the biggest territories among California Native American tribes. Not only was their land far-reaching, it probably had the best climate of any California tribal lands and more food than the tribe needed. Early explorers wrote in their journals about how intelligent, friendly, and good-natured the Chumash people were.

Chumash land stretched from San Luis Obispo in the north to Malibu Canyon in the south. Its western boundary was the Channel Islands in the Pacific Ocean; on the east it went inland to the edge of the San Joaquin Valley.

Chumash was not a name the tribe gave itself. It comes from the Coastal Chumash word "michumash", a name the Coastal Chumash had given to Santa Cruz Island people. It meant "island people". A man studying Native American languages gave the tribe this incorrect name when he wrote about the Chumash's six languages. From that time on, everyone has called this mainland tribe by the wrong name.

THE VILLAGE

A village was made up of several houses, a sweathouse, storage huts, a ceremonial building, a playing field, and a cemetery that was outside the village itself. Dirt paths ran between houses just as streets separate our houses today. Granaries, or storage houses, were usually near the chief's house so the chief could keep watch over the food inside them. The chief's granaries held food for old villagers, poor villagers, and for festival feasts, so it had to be protected from thieves.

Chumash villages along the coast were usually built on high ground near a freshwater stream running into the ocean.

The frame of a Chumash home. Tule mats were tied to the pole framework to form the walls.

Inland villages were also built near fresh water.

Family houses were round and had a domed roof. If you cut an orange in half and placed it flat side down, it would be the shape of a Chumash home. A frame for the home was made by bending several flexible poles and tying them together in the center. Tule mats were tied to the pole framework to form the walls of the house.

The floor of a house was dug into the ground a short way. Dirt that came from this shallow round hole was then tossed up onto the bottom of the tule mats which covered the framework of poles. This kept the wind out.

Mats made of rushes, grass, or tule were used for mattresses and for floors inside the home. These mats could also be used as walls to divide the house into more private rooms. Most houses held more than one family, but the families were related.

Spanish explorers greatly admired Chumash houses. In their journals they wrote of how large and light they were inside. Daylight came from the smoke hole in the center of the roof. Some houses could hold 70 people, according to the journals. One explorer said houses could be fifty feet across!

Every village had one or more sweathouses. Their floors were dug a bit deeper into the ground than those of houses. Poles were bent to the center like the ones in houses but were covered with earth instead of mats. The only way into a sweathouse was by climbing down a ladder from a hole in the top of the roof. The ladder was often made from a whale backbone.

The ceremonial building was nothing more than a roof held up by poles. It had no walls. The playing field was usually on a large level piece of village land. Its ground had been cleared of rocks and weeds and was hard and smooth from being used so much. Off to one side, but not too close to the village, was a cemetery.

VILLAGE LIFE

The largest and best house in the village belonged to the chief of the tribe. It held his family and often his sons' families. Some bigger villages had captains to help the chief. Sometimes the chiefs of smaller villages grouped together to form a council with one head chief. When that happened, a chief might be in charge of more than one village.

Chumash chiefs were not too powerful. Besides being war leaders, they were in charge of ceremonies and gave permission for other villages to hunt or gather food on village land. It was a chief's job to take care of ceremonial symbols and costumes and to entertain all visitors invited to ceremonies. Another of his jobs was to care for the poor people in his village.

A chief also had to handle all punishment in the village. If a thief stole items from another tribe member in the village, the chief made certain the thief returned all that was stolen. If this was not possible, the thief had to repay his victim with something of equal value. A chief might call for a fight to be fought between two quarreling villagers. The fighters might decide to use sweat-scrapers (sharp bones to scrape the skin clean) as weapons. Whoever drew blood from his enemy was the winner.

Only a chief could declare war and plan battles. The Chumash were friendly people, but certain insults could only be avenged by fighting. If a neighboring chief did not answer an invitation to a ceremony, or if another tribe trespassed on a tribe's land, the only way to pay back such insults was to fight.

Sometimes a problem could be solved by having a mock battle. Indian warriors came to these battles in full war paint, carrying bows and arrows, war clubs, and wooden spears. The Chumash threw feathers in the air. At that signal, war cries were sounded and one warrior would step forward to fire all his arrows into the enemy's line of warriors. This continued until one or more men were hurt or killed. The tribe or village holding the field when the battle was called off was declared winner.

A chief's job was for life. When a chief died, the next chief was usually a son of the dead leader. If the chief had no son, or the tribespeople did not trust the chief's son, a daughter could become chief. Once in a while, a sister of the chief could be chosen to lead the tribe.

A new bride was bought for a son with gifts from his parents to the bride's parents. Gifts often were animal skins, some beads, or a blanket. When a baby was born, it was a Chumash custom to flatten the infant's nose. The child was wrapped from feet to shoulders and placed on a board. The board hung like a sling from the mother's shoulders on her back. The baby stayed on the board, even for feedings. This left the mother's arms free to do her work. Babies were important to the tribe, but the work a woman did in gathering and cooking food was just as important.

In fact, so important were the jobs of young tribal adults,

that all training of Chumash children was left to the old men and women of the tribe. Old people not only had experience and wisdom to offer, they also had more time to teach children. Girls learned how to gather and prepare food, and how to make clothes and baskets. Old men taught the boys how to hunt and fish, and how to make and repair hunting and fishing equipment.

When a tribe member died, the body was carried to the ceremonial building. There, a huge fire was built. Singing and dancing went on through the night.

In the morning, the dead person was carried to the cemetery. After being tied in a bent position, the body was placed in the grave face down. All the dead person's personal items, such as eating bowls, pipes, and flint knives, were put in the grave also. A mourning ceremony was then held.

Every few years a mourning ceremony was repeated to honor all who had died. Usually this ceremony took place during a harvest festival.

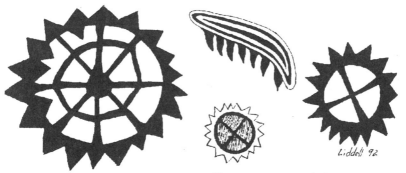

Some cave art of the Chumash.

FOOD

The Chumash people never went hungry. They did not even have to grow food; more than enough grew wild around them. They gathered a large variety of wild plant foods, fished their streams and the ocean, and hunted every animal, big or small. All this plenty was there for the taking.

The most important foods in their diet were acorns and fish. Fish could be roasted, eaten raw, dried, and wrapped in leaves and baked. Tribe members liked roasted fish best. Shark, bonito, sea bass, and halibut were all caught for food. Mollusks, such as clams, were eaten all year long. Crabs and lobsters were especially enjoyed

Acorns were gathered in the autumn and stored for winter meals. A whole village went to gather acorns. In a good harvest year, over two hundred pounds of acorns could come from one oak tree. Large huts were built to hold the huge amounts of acorns harvested. Read Chapter One to see how the acorn flour was prepared.

Summer was the best time to gather food plants. Some of them were eaten fresh, but most were dried and stored for winter meals. Berries of the California laurel were roasted and eaten. Each summer, tribe members enjoyed eating ripened wild blackberries, strawberries, elderberries, and more. Pine nuts were eaten summer or winter. At the beginning of the rainy season in November, watercress, wild celery, and amaranth were gathered.

Tribal women had a clever way of getting sugar for their meals. The sweet droppings of aphids and whiteflies were found on carrizo grass. Large amounts of the grass were cut and beaten in winnowing baskets. The droppings, called honeydew, would collect on the bottom of the winnowing basket. The women carefully gathered honeydew by rolling it into sticky balls which could then be eaten for dessert.

Soap plant was used in many ways. The bulb was roasted and eaten; the green, unripe bulb made good soap for washing, and its dry leaves could be shredded and bound together to make brushes. Crushed soap plant was used as a fish poison. A small bit of the poison was sprinkled on the water in quiet spots of a stream. Fish became confused when they ate the drug and could be picked up right out of the water!

HUNTING AND FISHING

Chumash men were excellent hunters and fishermen. A lot of their success was because of the very fine hunting weapons and fish traps they designed. Chumash bows are a good example of this. There were two kinds of bows used by tribal hunters. The simplest bow was a self-bow, meaning it was only made of a piece of wood. Nothing was added. It was from 3½ to 4½ feet long and made out of elderberry or juniper wood. Used to kill small animals, this kind of bow was left unstrung until needed. Hunters became so good at stringing it, they could actually string one while running.

The finest bow Chumash men made was sinew-backed. It was needed for hunting large animals and for fighting battles. It was under four feet long and usually made of toyon or elder wood. After rough shaping, the bow wood was heated in hot water, curved at the middle, and then curved again at the tip ends. Tar or glue made of tree pitch was put on the whole bow. Strips of sinew (elastic-like animal tendon) were laid lengthwise on top of the glue. More sinew was wound around the middle of the bow to give it strength.

Self-arrow was the name given to a one-piece, all wood arrow with no arrowhead attached to the end. The tip was hardened by putting it in fire. These arrows were used for contests or for killing small animals. Arrows made to kill larger animals and for use in battles were longer, stronger, and harder to make. Carrizo cane was used for the shaft. It was dried first, then straightened on a hot, grooved straightening stone. Placing feathers at the opposite end of an arrow from the point was called fletching. Great care was taken in attaching feathers so the arrow would fly straight. Arrowheads were usually made from chert, a stone which flaked to a sharp point when broken. Sometimes men traded for obsidian to use in making arrowheads.

Slingshots could kill birds and small animals. Traps and snares were used to capture some game. When a hunter stalked deer, he often wore a deerhead on his own head. The closer hunters could get to deer, the better chance they had to kill one. It has been told that Chumash men hunted deer with poisoned arrows, but no one knows this for sure.

Chumash men had many ways to catch fish. They used traps for lobsters, nets for crabs. Sardines were caught with dip nets. Dip nets were about three feet around at the top and had a drawstring to pull to keep the sardines from

Hunter wearing deerhead camouflage.

getting away. Seine, drag and gill nets were made by Chumash fishermen. Netting cord came from sea grass or milkweed fibers. Although both men and women worked on making nets and fixing torn ones, only the men fished.

Hooks for line fishing could be made from bent cactus needles, shell, bone, or wood. Spears, harpoons, even big clubs were used to catch larger fish and animals like seals and sea lions. Smaller fish were caught in seines and dip nets of twisted plant fiber.

Fishing in streams was different from ocean fishing. Often a weir, which was a low stone wall with a narrow opening in the center of it, was built across a stream. A trap was placed in the opening, catching fish as they moved upstream. Nets and hooks were also used in streams to catch fish.

Plank canoe, called tomol, which was used to cross ocean channels to channel islands.

BOATS

Chumash plank boats were so excellent, they deserve to have a whole section written about them. Chumash boatmakers built the only sea-going canoe on the North American continent. Some experts feel this was one of the finest boats ever built by Native Americans. It was used by the tribe to reach fishing grounds and making the long trip across the Santa Barbara Channel to the channel islands. Chumash people called the boat "tomol".

Tomol was made of wood planks. The exact way of building the canoe was a secret known only to boatmakers. This secret was passed on to young men especially chosen to be trained by old boatmakers of the tribe. It was a great honor to build boats, and boatbuilders were treated with great respect by the whole tribe. Only rich tribal leaders could own a boat. If someone was rich enough to own one of the plank canoes, he was allowed to wear a bear-skin cape which hung down to the waist. The cape told everyone how important a man the boat owner was.

Wood for each boat was carefully chosen. It had to be free of knots and the grain of the wood had to be straight. Planks were split from the logs, using a whale rib as a wedge. The men used only shells and sharp flint rocks to shape each plank. Sharkskin was used for sandpaper to smooth the flat side of the boards. The planks were then sewn together with very strong plant-fiber thread. Every joint (where the planks fit together) was covered with pitch or tar. All tomols were painted red. Some were decorated with small shells.

Tomols were light in weight and very fast in the water. They went from ten feet to thirty feet in length and were narrow across. A canoe was designed so each end came to a point. The building of these boats was never hurried and each was carefully made. For this reason it took between two and six months to finish a boat. The plank canoe was steered and moved by two six-foot double-bladed oars.

Boatbuilders were proud of their craft and formed a union or guild, just for boatmakers. Other tribal craftsmen formed unions or guilds for their crafts. By organizing in such groups, men and women found they could begin to make more items than they needed, so they had fine products to offer for trade, or for sale. That is why the Chumash tribe was one of the richest of the California tribes.

TOOLS, UTENSILS, AND BASKETS

Chumash craftsmen used objects from nature as tools. Sharp stones and shells became knives. Sticks became digging tools. Sharp, strong whale bones became wedges. Shell and bone were made into tools for crafting objects. Needles, fish hooks, and harpoon heads were made from animal or bird bones. One interesting tool was a swordfish bill used as a sweathouse skin scraper! With such simple tools the crafts-men made everything the tribe needed for daily life.

Some of the finest stone objects crafted by Chumash people

were made of steatite. Steatite, or soapstone, came from Catalina Island. The Chumash traveled in plank canoes to get it. Soapstone conducted heat quite well, so cooking pans like frying skillets (comals) were made from it. It was also used for bowls and jars (ollas). Soapstone was a soft stone, easy to decorate, easy to shape, and easy to smooth its surfaces.

Very sharp arrowheads were made of a flaking stone called chert. Blades for knives came from sharp-edged chert. Sometimes the Chumash got obsidian by trading with northern tribes. Obsidian is a volcanic "glass" used by California Native Americans to make arrowheads which were tougher than chert arrowheads.

Sandstone was used to make large storage bowls. Wooden plates and bowls for eating were made from the roots of oak and alder trees. The plates and bowls were so well-crafted that explorers described them as looking like they had been made with lathe saws. Mortars and pestles carved of wood were used by the women to grind seeds and grains. Boxes made of small planks and finished with shell decorations were also written about in explorers' journals.

Chumash women made superb baskets. Explorers and white settlers collected them, they were so beautiful.

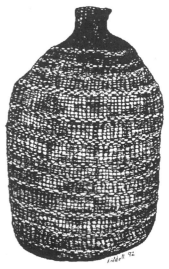

They were made for carrying and storing water, for collecting bulbs and roots, and for straining sifting, cooking, and storing food. Baskets were also made to be used as plates and bowls, for storing blankets, and for hundreds of other uses.

Chumash baskets were made of willow branches, rushes, cattails, and tule reed. Most of these plants

Twined basket water container.

grew nearby. The plants were gathered and spread out to dry. The dried plants then were tied in bundles and stored until needed. Finished baskets were tan colored. Sumac shoots were used for white decorations and fern root for black decorations on the baskets. It was thought that geometric patterns decorating many baskets had some meaning to the basketmaker.

Tar, or asphaltum, was used to seal baskets, so they could carry water. Some coiled baskets were so tightly woven, however, they could hold water without being sealed.

Baskets used as strainers or sifters were loosely twined and used as we use flour sifters today. One of the most interesting baskets was a hopper. It had no bottom and was glued to the top of a rock mortar. This kept small grains and seeds from blowing away as they were being ground by a pestle.

TRADING

Chumash people made most of the shell-bead money used by tribes throughout the California territory. The beads were made from Olivella shells found on Chumash beaches. These shell beads were strung in lengths measured by the distance around a human hand.

A hard-working tribe like the Chumash tribe had many fine products to offer in trade to other tribes. Their trading was divided into three areas: inland, coast, and island. Inland tribelets came to the coast for fresh and dried fish, shellfish, baskets, steatite, chipped stone points for tools and arrows, stone for tools, and for carved wooden bowls and jars. They brought with them from their desert homes, blankets, a fire-hardened pottery the Coastal Chumash really liked, small balls of bright red powder used for body and rock painting, elk, deer, and antelope meat, and salt.

Tribelets on the mainland wanted from the island people beads, shell jewelry, steatite, otter and seal skins, chert

Liddell 42

Flint knife with attached wooden handle.

knives, baskets, and sea lion meat. In return the islanders needed acorns, pine nuts, deer and rabbit skins, deer antlers for tools, bows and arrows, baskets, and obsidian.

CLOTHING

The first writings of how Chumash people dressed were by explorer Juan Cabrillo in 1542. He wrote how the Indians dressed in skins and wore their hair very long and tied back at the neck. In 1775, the Chumash tribe was described as wearing no clothing, except for special occasions. Some tribal members had their noses and ears pierced.

It was written that for cool weather the important men wore large capes of animal skins. Since the explorer who wrote this probably had been seeing only tribe leaders, he must have been speaking of rich men and boat owners. He did write that only the "captain" (chief) could wear a cape that hung to the ground. It was noted that men carried nettings around their waists to hold small objects they needed to carry with them. Some of the men plucked out their beards with clamshell tweezers to keep themselves clean-shaven. The women wore their hair in bangs, with the rest hanging loose and long in the back.

For clothing on cooler days, the women wore knee-length buckskin skirts, one in front and one in back. The edges of the skirts were fringed, and ornaments like snail shells and pieces of abalone shells hung from the fringe. Sometimes the skirts were stained bright red or white.

Some women wore pieces of soft deerskin wrapped around their waists like a wrap-around skirt. Ankle-length decorated skirts were also worn. Headbands and cloaks were decorated with colored shells of red, black, and white. Women covered their heads with small woven trays or baskets shaped like beanie-caps.

While the rich and more powerful people wore furs, the common people wore clothes of grass and shredded tree bark. Willow, cottonwood, or sycamore bark seemed the most popular. The inner bark was cut away in strips and shredded into fibers. These fibers were then woven into fabric. Bits of tar were attached to the bottoms of grass skirts to keep them down when the wind was blowing.

Woman with basket hat and face-painting.

Special clothing was worn for ceremonies. Women wore antelope-hide skirts and thin tubes of clam shells in their noses. At ritual dances, important men wore net skirts woven from vegetable fiber. They were hemmed with hanging feathers. Ritual headgear was beautiful. The feather headbands were made from the orange quills of a bird, the red-shafted flicker. Hundreds of these feathers were used for each band. For one power dance, the bear doctor wore a costume of black-bear skin.

Strands of shell bead, bone, and steatite necklaces were worn by both men and women. Much body painting was done. Each village had its own designs for body decorations. Then, when there were dances, the village groups could be told from one another. Face-painting patterns were usually stripes or zigzags. Body paints were for decoration, but they also protected the skin from the sun.

RELIGION AND BELIEFS

Chumash people believed in supernatural forces. They believed humans were important because they were the ones who kept a balance between good and evil. Chumash legends tell of three worlds, flat and piled up like three coins. The top world was where the most powerful gods lived. The middle world was our earth. Before man came to this middle world, the First People lived there until a terrible flood washed them away. It was believed that dark and evil beings, who wished to hurt humans, lived in the lower world.

In order to protect themselves, the Chumash counted on help from the tribe's shamans. Shamans had ways to speak to spirits. It was shamans who were with people at important moments such as birth and death. A shaman named children. It was felt they could predict the future and the weather. One of the most important shamans was the one who cured sickness. Herbs, smoke, singing, and dancing were used to cure.

Dances were performed to please the powers. Certain dances were directed at animals they felt held power over them that was greater than their own. Two of those dances were the Bear Dance and the Swordfish Dance. Each dance had certain steps that had to be done exactly the same way each time.

GAMES AND MUSIC

Having been blessed with good food and good weather, the Chumash people had time for pleasant things like games, singing, and dancing. Every village had a playing field. Games of kickball, shinny, archery and hoop and pole were played there. Hoop and pole was played by rolling a stone disc on the ground. Players tried to spear through a hole in the center of the disc. Shinny was played with curved wooden

A shaman in full ceremonial costume. Dance skirt is of milkweed fiber strings with eagle down twisted into the string. Feathers are tied to lower ends of strings.

Liddell 92

bats that looked like modern-day hockey sticks. A wooden ball was batted about as players tried to reach a goal at one end of the field.

Both women and men enjoyed games of chance. Dice were made from one half a decorated walnut shell and were thrown on a basket tray. Shell-bead money and other valuables were used for bets.

Singing was a favorite pastime of the tribespeople. Songs could be serious, religious ones, or funny. Visitors were entertained with the funny songs. Babies were sung to sleep with lullabies. Children had their own songs, too. Some songs told stories of the tribe.

Rhythm instruments were played along with the singing. Strangely, no drum was used by the tribe. Split-stick clappers, deer-hoof rattles, and bullroarers were usually used. The bullroarer was a short plank of wood swung fast enough around the head of a player to make a low buzzing sound.

A flute made of hollow bone was the only musical instrument that could actually play a tune. It had several holes on its side and was open at both ends. Whistles were made from cane or bird and animal bones and were sometimes tied together to make several different tones.

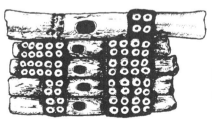

Five bone whistle, glued together with tar and decorated with tiny shell beads.

Whistle made of mountain lion bone with abalone shells inlaid into the end.

HISTORY

Anthropologists are people who study ancient ways of life. Archaeologists study the belongings, the things of ancient peoples' lives. In their studies, both have had to depend on the journals and diaries of explorers to piece together facts about early Chumash tribal life.

There were five California missions in Chumash territory. Mission life was readily accepted by the Chumash tribelets. Their easy-going manner helped them adjust to changes. Tribe members worked hard for the Franciscan monks who ran the missions. In doing this, the Chumash people simply forgot their old ways of living. In the late 1800s, people finally became curious about long-ago tribal life. By that time, most of the people who had lived in tribal villages and might have remembered how it was, were either very old or dead. Many of the facts about early tribal life have been lost forever.

Some historians believe there may have been up to 22,000 Chumash people living on their land before White people came. White people brought strange sicknesses, like measles and small pox, with them. Those Chumash not killed by disease or White men's guns were finally placed on U.S. government reservations to live. Until the 1960s, the government handled every part of their lives. In 1970 only 40 Chumash were counted in California, and none of those were of all-Chumash blood . . . a very sad ending to such a fine, intelligent, hard-working group of people.

Examples of Chumash cave art.

Liddell 92

44

OUTLINE OF CHUMASH TRIBE

I. Introduction
    A. Description of people
    B. Territory
    C. Meaning of name Chumash

II. The village
    A. Kinds of buildings
        1. House description and how it was built
        2. Description of sweathouse
        3. Ceremonial enclosure
    B. Other places in village
        1. Playing field
        2. Cemetery

III. Village life
    A. Chief
        1. How chosen
        2. Duties
    B. Marriages and children
        1. How husbands and wives were chosen
        2. A baby's early life
        3. Training of children by grandparents
        4. Jobs of young adults – food gathering
    C. Death
        1. Rituals performed
        2. Mourning, or image, ceremony

IV. Food
    A. Most important foods
        1. Acorns
        2. Fish
    B. Plant foods
        1. Fresh plants, berries, and nuts
        2. Dried foods

C. Sugar and sweets
D. The soap plant uses
V. Hunting and fishing
   A. Hunting weapons
      1. Bows and arrows
      2. Slingshots
   B . Fishing
      1. Traps
      2. Nets
      3. Hook and line fishing
      4. Sea fishing
VI. Boats
   A. Plank boats (tomols)
      1. Importance of boatmakers in the tribe
      2. Kind of wood used
      3. Materials and tools used in building boats
      4. "Sewing" of planks
      5. Description of tomol
      6. Length of time to make boat
      7. How boat was steered and where it went
VII. Tools, utensils, and baskets
   A. Natural objects used as tools
   B. Stone tools
   C. Baskets
      1. Kinds and uses of baskets
      2. Materials used to make baskets
VIII. Trading
   A. Shell-bead money
   B. Products traded
   C. Products wanted by coastal and mainland people

IX. Clothing
    A. Men
    B. Women
    C. Rich tribal members
    D. Clothing of common people
    E. Ceremonial costumes
        1. Decorations
        2. Jewelry
        3. Body paints
X. Religion and beliefs
    A. Legends
    B. Shamans
    C. Dances
XI. Games and music
    A. Games
        1. Outdoor games on playing field
        2. Games of chance
    B. Music
        1. Songs and singing
        2. Rhythm instruments
        3. Flute
XII. History
    A. Explorers' journals
    B. Mission life
    C. Living on reservations

GLOSSARY

AWL: a sharp, pointed tool used for making small holes in leather or wood

CEREMONY: a meeting of people to perform formal rituals for a special reason; like an awards ceremony to hand out trophies to those who earned honors

CHERT: rock which can be chipped off, or flaked, into pieces with sharp edges

COILED: a way of weaving baskets which looks like the basket is made of rope coils woven together

DIAMETER: the length of a straight line through the center of a circle

DOWN: soft, fluffy feathers

DROUGHT: a long period of time without water

DWELLING: a building where people live

FLETCHING: attaching feathers to the back end of an arrow to make the arrow travel in a straight line

GILL NET: a flat net hanging vertically in water to catch fish by their heads and gills

GRANARIES: basket-type storehouses for grains and nuts

HERITAGE: something passed down to people from their long-ago relatives

LEACHING: washing away a bitter taste by pouring water through foods like acorn meal

MORTAR: flat surface of wood or stone used for the grinding of grains or herbs with a pestle

PARCHING:	to toast or shrivel with dry heat
PESTLE:	a small stone club used to mash, pound, or grind in a mortar
PINOLE:	flour made from ground corn
INDIAN RESERVATION:	land set aside for Native Americans by the United States government
RITUAL:	a ceremony that is always performed the same way
SEINE NET:	a net which hangs vertically in the water, encircling and trapping fish when it is pulled together
SHAMAN:	tribal religious men or women who use magic to cure illness and speak to spirit-gods
SINEW:	stretchy animal tendons
STEATITE:	a soft stone (soapstone) mined on Catalina Island by the Gabrielino tribe; used for cooking pots and bowls
TABOO:	something a person is forbidden to do
TERRITORY:	land owned by someone or by a group of people
TRADITION:	the handing down of customs, rituals, and belief, by word of mouth or example, from generation to generation
TREE PITCH:	a sticky substance found on evergreen tree bark
TWINING:	a method of weaving baskets by twisting fibers, rather than coiling them around a support fiber

NATIVE AMERICAN WORDS
WE KNOW AND USE

PLANTS AND TREES
hickory
pecan
yucca
mesquite
saguaro

ANIMALS
caribou
chipmunk
cougar
jaguar
opossum
moose

STATES
Dakota – friend
Ohio – good river
Minnesota – waters that
    reflect the sky
Oregon – beautiful water
Nebraska – flat water
Arizona
Texas

FOODS
avocado
hominy
maize (corn)
persimmon
tapioca
succotash

GEOGRAPHY
bayou – marshy body of
    water
savannah – grassy plain
pasadena – valley

WEATHER
blizzard
Chinook (warm, dry wind)

FURNITURE
hammock

HOUSE
wigwam
wickiup
tepee
igloo

INVENTIONS
toboggan

BOATS
canoe
kayak

OTHER WORDS
caucus – group meeting
mugwump – loner politician
squaw – woman
papoose – baby

CLOTHING
moccasin
parka
mukluk – slipper
poncho

BIBLIOGRAPHY

Cressman, L. S. *Prehistory of the Far West.* Salt Lake City, Utah: University of Utah Press, 1977.

Geiger, Maynard, O.F.M., Ph.D. *The Indians of Mission Santa Barbara.* Santa Barbara, CA 93105: Franciscan Fathers, 1986.

Heizer, Robert F., volume editor. *Handbook of North American Indians; California, volume 8.* Washington, D.C.: Smithsonian Institute, 1978.

Heizer, Robert F. and Elsasser, Albert B. *The Natural World of the California Indians.* Berkeley and Los Angeles, CA; London, England: University of California Press, 1980.

Heizer, Robert F. and Whipple, M.A.. *The California Indians.* Berkeley and Los Angeles, CA; London, England: University of California Press, 1971.

Heuser, Iva. *California Indians.* PO Box 352, Camino, CA 95709: Sierra Media Systems, 1977.

Macfarlen, Allen and Paulette. *Handbook of American Indian Games.* 31 E. 2nd Street, Mineola, N.Y. 11501: Dover Publications, 1985.

Murphey, Edith Van Allen. *Indian Uses of Native Plants.* 603 W. Perkins Street, Ukiah, CA 95482: Mendocino County Historical Society, © renewal, 1987.

National Geographic Society. *The World of American Indians.* Washington, DC: National Geographic Society reprint, 1989.

Tunis, Edwin. *Indians.* 2231 West 110th Street, Cleveland, OH: The World Publishing Company, 1959.

Credits:
The Pollard Group, Inc., Tacoma, Washington 98409
Dona McAdam, Mac on the Hill, Seattle, Washington 98109

Acknowledgements:
Richard Buchen, Research Librarian, Braun Library,
Southwest Museum